Illumen
Autumn 2024

Edited by
Tyree Campbell

Illumen
Autumn 2024

Edited by Tyree Campbell

Cover art "Star Rise" by Brian Quinn
Cover design by Laura Givens

Vol. XXII, No. 1   Autumn 2024
Illumen [ISSN: 1558-9714] is published quarterly on the 1st days of January, April, July, and October in the United States of America by Hiraeth Publishing, P.O. Box 1248, Tularosa, NM 88352. Copyright 2024 by Hiraeth Publishing. All rights revert to authors and artists upon publication except as noted in selected individual contracts. Nothing may be reproduced in whole or in part without written permission from the authors and artists. Any similarity between places and persons mentioned in the fiction or semi-fiction and real places or persons living or dead is coincidental. Writers and artists guidelines are available online at www.albanlake.com/guidelines. Guidelines are also available upon request from Hiraeth Publishing, P.O. Box 1248, Tularosa, NM 88352, if request is accompanied by a SASE #10 envelope with a 60-cent US stamp. Editor: Tyree Campbell. Subscriptions: $28 for one year [4 issues], $54 for two years [8 issues]. Single copies $10.00 postage paid in the United States. Subscriptions to Canada: $32 for one year, $54 for two years. Single copies $12.00 postage paid to Canada. U.S. and Canadian subscribers remit in U.S. funds. All other countries inquire about rates.

New from Terrie Leigh Relf!!
Postcards From Space

Terrie Leigh Relf loves sending and receiving postcards from the four corners of the universe—and beyond! Postcards tell a story. They are mementos from friends and family—and from total strangers—and provide a glimpse into life's journeys, observations, and adventures.

Here are some messages on postcards from space, found aboard a derelict craft that crashed on an arid, lifeless world. The OSPS (Outer Space Postal Service) has delivered these messages to Terrie, who now presents them to you. This is what it is like out there.

https://www.hiraethsffh.com/product-page/postcards-from-space-by-terrie-leigh-relf

A Little Help, Please

In the world of the small indie press we fight a never-ending battle for attention to our work, as writers and in publishing. Here's an example: big publishers [you know who they are] have gobs of $$$ that they can devote to advertising and marketing. Here at Hiraeth Publishing, our advertising budget consists of the deposits for whatever soda bottles and aluminum cans we can find alongside the highways. Anti-littering laws make our task even more difficult . . . ☺

That's where YOU come in. YOU are our best promoter. YOU are the one who can tell others about us. Just send 'em to our website, tell them about our store. That's all. Just that.

Of course, we don't mind if you talk us up. We're pretty good, you know. We have some award-winning and award-nominated writers and artists, plus other voices well-deserving to be heard [not everyone wins awards, right?] but our publications are read-worthy nevertheless.

That number once again is:

www.hiraethsffh.com

Friend us on Facebook at Hiraeth Publish and follow us on Twitter at

@HiraethPublish1

Contents

Features
20	Illumen Interviews Christian Dickinson
32-34	Featured Poet: Dawn McCormack
38	The Richard E. Schell Page

Poems
10	Autumn by Sandy DeLuca
13	Cup of Lava by Johanna Haas
14	Afterimages by Marcie Lynn Tentchoff
16	A Throne of Stone and Honey by Gary Every
18	Slumber Party by Hannah Marshall
19	Will-o'-the-Wisp by Christian Dickinson
24	Getting Close to Thanatos by Shawn Vimislicky
27	Relics by Lee Clark Zumpe
30	The Swamp Witch's Lament by Marcie Lynn Tentchoff
31	A Scan of the Beating Heart by Hannah Marshall
35	not what you expect by Lee Clark Zumpe
39	neighborhood great by Denise Noe Dissonance by Amy Grech
40	Tickets to the Apocalypse by Kendall Evans & David C. Kopaska-Merkel
42	Identified by Marcie Lynn Tentchoff
43	Lavinia and the Moon by Lee Clark Zumpe

Illustrations
12	Autumn by Sandy DeLuca
23	Drought Garden by Denny Marshall

SUBSCRIBE TO ILLUMEN!!

We'll be glad you did...
So will you.
Here's the link:

https://www.hiraethsffh.com/product-page/illumen-1

Support the small independent press!

You're not afraid of a little poetry, are you?

The Miseducation of the Androids
By William Landis

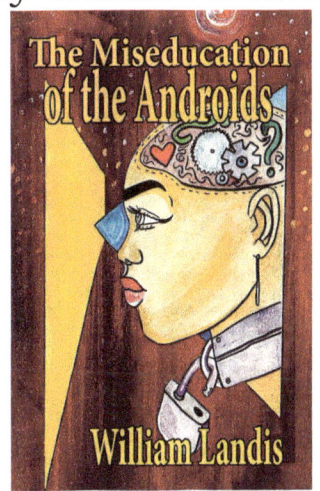

What happens when androids confront concepts inconsistent with their programming? William Landis examines this question by means of flash fiction and haiku that you will find pithy, poignant, and amusing.

William Landis is a science fiction poet from North Carolina. He is a graduate of North Carolina A&T State University, completing both undergraduate, and graduate work in agriculture. He is currently working on a vermicomposting project, and he is an Army reserve engineer officer. He enjoys running, writing, reading, and exploring new places.

Order a copy here: https://www.hiraethsffh.com/product-page/miseducation-of-the-androids-by-william-landis

Midnight Comes Early

By Marcie Lynn Tentchoff

Marcie Lynn Tentchoff lives on the west coast of Canada, in a forest of brambles and evergreens far too densely tangled to form the setting for any but the darkest of fairy tales. She writes poetry and stories that tiptoe worriedly along the border of speculation and horror, and is an active member of both the Science Fiction & Fantasy Poetry Association and the Horror Writers Association. Marcie is an Aurora Award winner, and her work has been either nominated, short, or long-listed for Stoker, Rhysling, and British Fantasy awards. She is very much involved in middle grade and YA media, and edits Spaceports & Spidersilk, a magazine aimed at readers from 8-9 up to (and past!) 89. When she is not involved with the practice of placing and editing words on a page, she teaches creative writing and acting for a performing arts studio.

Order a copy here...

https://www.hiraethsffh.com/product-page/midnight-comes-early-by-marcie-lynn-tentchoff

When Autumn Comes
Sandy DeLuca

I go back to my grandmother's house
in murky dreams,
peek into rooms forbidden
when I was a child,
speak to guests who visited long
after I was put down to sleep,
gaze through rain-soaked windows
at dead leaves and pumpkins
splattered on the walk.

Tabby cats huddle close,
wash each other,
lover's kisses;
they know secrets whispered at
the kitchen table,
by women with gnarled fingers
and rosaries tucked in their belts,
slicing October apples
with knives as sharp as Strega curses.

Oil and water mingled to release
demons that hovered by
by the chimney;
playing cards revealed
deeds plotted by their men
over wine and cigarette smoke;
sons laid out in caskets
before youth faded;
daughters tainted by sailors
met in the city.

So many rooms to discover...

What hides in the attic,
or in the basement?
corpses and vials of
dried blood...

bottles lines up on dusty shelves;
potions conjured on the day
of my birth.

The divine
mixed with the immoral;
they all look the same...

my legacy—
to taste every drop.

Apocalypse is a powerful, lyrical compendium of dooms (the plural is deliberate) befalling myriad beings ranging from proto-human to utterly alien. Some of these beings are us, and our enemies, ourselves. There is a (un) healthy dose of hostile invaders on which to blame our downfalls

—F.J. Bergmann, Editor of *Star*Line*.

Ordering Link:
Print: https://www.hiraethsffh.com/product-page/this-is-apocalypse-by-john-c-mannone

Autumn by Sandy DeLuca

Cup of Lava
Johanna Haas

Ella dips her cup into the river of lava.
It ceases being magma when it reaches the surface.
She knows strange silicate minerals form most
    of its flow,
Feldspars, olivine, amphibole, mica, and quartz.
She knows it glows hotter than any oven.
It will never be as magnificent as it is today.
She knows.

A cup of lava, of earth at its simplest.
She knows it is prime and ready to become new-born.
She seeks the silica-fresh, untouched, smooth,
Pouring her dip slowly into her vast basin of water,
Spaghetti strings of obsidian,
(And chunks of basalt after the water warms.)
A rarity for the rock-eaters.
She knows.

Afterimages
Marcie Lynn Tentchoff

He takes her picture,
down beside
the mill pond,
laughing softly at
the grass green stains
on her white skirt.

Flash

She smiles there
beside the water,
fingers trailing
through the water lilies,
tossing playful drops,
and glances
back at him.

Flash

She reaches out,
still smiling,
as a bubble
rises from the
cloudy depths
and

Flash

it pops, her fingertips
turn rainbow hued
and glimmer in
the noonday sun
then

Flash

the colors swirl
and spread
and run in patterns
up her arms
and further...

Flash

Her smile lingers,
gentle as the
gentle breeze,
then nothing more,
save pictures on
a camera disc
she'll never view.

A Throne of Stone and Honey
Gary Every

Her thoughts were distant, money on her lips,
while honey filled her hips as she walked.
The men's necks would roll as they gawked,
watching as she strolled, admiring the way
    her stride flowed.
The queen perched regally atop her throne of stone,
a seat built upon a pile of bones, composed of
skeletons from fallen faithful followers,
    forlorn lonely soldiers,
and lovestruck generals seeking gory glories.
The queen did not grieve a single tombstone.
Many men wished to hold her close,
believing her heart would taste like honey,
believing her smile shone like rainbows,
unaware of her underworld soul
filled with cemetery storms and teasing crows.
A few reckless men had tasted a single blissful kiss
paying for their romantic dances with necklaces of
gold and glittering gemstones.
What the queen craved was not love and affection
but the eternity of history, the fame and erection
of oversized monuments.
As she aged, she raged, ruling with an iron fist
    and fear,
knowing that someday soon
her reign would be a thing of yesteryear
and her passing would not bring a single tear.

The newest from G. O. Clark!!!
Mindscapes

G. O. Clark takes on the future in this riveting collection of poetic observations about life, the Universe, and everything else. He takes you up mountains and down valleys, and always makes you wonder about what's happening and what will happen (if we aren't careful).

Ordering links:
Print: https://www.hiraethsffh.com/product-page/mindscapes-by-g-o-clark
ePub: https://www.hiraethsffh.com/product-page/mindscapes-by-g-o-clark-2
PDF: https://www.hiraethsffh.com/product-page/mindscapes-by-g-o-clark-1

Slumber Party
Hannah Marshall

Outside the basement room, the hills shrill green,
the cows valley in the muddy creek.
Seven girls peek between pillows at an iron face,
at asteroids and the force of death,
body against body. Ligament music.
All night long we whisper as outside
the scheduled horror of camellias
bloom through cow skull, eye socket petaling pink,
perfect symmetry. Toothless profanity.
We are gathered by our mothers in the morning
and plod wearily to church, hymnal pages sibilant
against our fathers' dry hands, songs, turnings,
a tomorrow of lyric. There is no unlearning fear,
the thin edges of our child-skin bent bright
against the blank mirror of the window,
outside the burning bush filled with birds
and the cries our muscles have buried.
Inside, we hold knives and burnt popcorn.
Inside, shadows fold into hexagonal labyrinths.
The spirals of Gilgamesh
and the long woods of moon. I still wake sometimes,
afraid of that gray face. Afraid of the bridge,
the water blinding blue, even as the sky burns.

Will-o'-the-Wisp
Christian Dickinson

Hush! Hush!—make not the slightest stir nor sound.
Foul spirits roam the marsh as well as fair;
We hover through the fog and filthy air
To give to men all joys that may be found.
Is gold your heart's most intimate desire?
Or do you find your bliss in beauty's arms?
Would you a body free from nature's harms?
The skill to call down thunder—summon fire?

We like your look and know your worth quite well,
So much deserving of these mystic gifts.
Then take your prize—their worth your right exclaims!
Just step a little closer to our flames…
Yet closer…closer…there! The marshland shifts—
And matins' toll will sound an extra knell.

**Winner, 2nd Place Elgin Award 2018!!!
Astropoetry by Christina Sng!**

https://www.hiraethsffh.com/product-page/astropoetry-by-christina-sng

Illumen Interviews Christian Dickinson

How long have you been writing poetry?

Poetry is actually a relatively recent venture for me. I have been interested in fiction-writing for years, but it has only been in the last 2 or 3 that I have really committed to producing poetry in a committed way. A friend of mine who operates an editing service once posted this comment: If you want to become a great fiction writer, become a great poet first. The idea being that writing poetry forces you to fine-tune your craft skills at the very minutest levels – grammar, syntax, vocabulary, image, idea – they all have to be executed as precisely as possible in order for a poem to "work".

What do you try to say or convey in your poetry?

As a person of faith, my goal is to use all my writing to convey or exemplify a system of belief in the Divine and / or notions of traditional moral virtue. As a lover of the Western and English Canon, a lot of my writing is a reworking of mythology and more traditional forms. I want to show people how engaging and enjoyable traditional, set forms can be, and demonstrate that there is an alternative to free-verse that should not be thought of as obsolete or outdated. I also want the poetry I write to be an exploration of the powers of the imagination to create fantastical realities – something I have stolen from the Romantics.

Where did you learn to write scifaiku?

If you are talking about speculative poetry more generally, I learned from just reading a great deal of traditional form poetry. I teach English Literature at the college level, so I really immersed myself in the older forms. I am also incredibly blessed to have one or two very good friends who are also writers that have agreed to do a lot of beta reading for me!

Do you write poetry other than genre poetry? If so, what kind?

Absolutely – right now, I am working in basically two different categories – one is genre fiction, and the other is adaptations / reimaginings of mythical or ancient texts, including Scripture. I actually just finished the second volume of a two-volume collection of poetry, in which I took the Biblical book of Psalms and reworked them into English-Form "Shakespearean" Sonnets ["Sonnets from the Psalms" – available on Amazon!]. The goal right now is to write a collection of poems in each of the major forms, starting from the Sonnet, and then working all the way up to an Epic – we'll see how far I get!

Whose poetry has influenced you the most?

If I had to choose just one writer whose poems are a beacon for me, it would have to be Alfred Lord Tennyson. The music of his lines is absolutely unparalleled, and many of his subjects are of course exactly what I want mine to be – reimaginings of mythology and legend. For this collection in particular, I was also heavily influenced by Lovecraft's "Fungi from Yuggoth" – that book is a collection of Petrarchan Sonnets that create a bizarre image with a mind-bending gut-punch at the end. I try to do that with all these creature poems.

I also have a great love for Robert Browning's poetic monologues – the way he is able to plumb the psychology of a character and the world they inhabit with just his or her internal monologue is uncredible. I was also inspired by a biography about Browning which explained that he was basically one of history's greatest auto-didacts. Instead of going to college, he spent four years reading his father's entire library; this is what gave his poetry the philosophical depth that it has.

Who is your favorite poet?

Either Tennyson or Robert Browning. Beyond that, I would have to choose individual works like *The Canterbury Tales, The Faerie Queene, Paradise Lost,* etc.,

What/who is your main inspiration?

C. S. Lewis, J. R. R. Tolkien – the way that they were able to so seamlessly blend together their faith and their works of the imagination without coming off as "preachy" is something I will spend the rest of my life attempting to accomplish. I also have to give a big "thank you" to my dear friend and professorial colleague Geoffrey Reiter – he has encouraged me in my writing more than anyone else, has been an example of industrious commitment to the craft, and has been very generous in his feedback to the work I have sent him over the years.

What poetry magazines do you read/contribute to?

I mostly subscribe to "Fantasy and Science Fiction" and "Asimov's". I contribute to a number of magazines, but the ones I submit to most often have been "Spectral Realms", "ParABnormal", and "The Mythic Circle".

Drought Garden
By Denny Marshall

Getting Close to Thanatos
Shawn Vimislicky

There arrived an unexpected messenger
   descending between two receding clouds,
   and following her was a glowing black crackling
lightning.
This waif of Darkness gracefully landed and folded in
   her mighty wings of glossy feathering.
Very lean and darkly alluring in the dress of a gothic
   temptress, she quietly told me that when young
   I was marked and kissed by a great force of
Darkness.
I was mistakenly separated and temporarily lost,
   but now I must say so long to the Eros driven
   throng, and go journey to where I truly belong.
She then clapped her hands six times and kissed
   my wrinkled brow, and I do not know how,
   but the glowing black crackling lightning
   became my mighty journey strong Death Wings.

On my way I reacquainted myself with disease and
   decay, two true friends to my kind, and harmless to
   my body and mind.
Eventually, I spotted and landed on blackened brown
   ground.
From flowers noxious I lapped up dew phosphorus,
   and enjoyed tasting green frothing sour nectar.
Much later, after further descending more levels of
   darkness, I landed near a diseased forest.
Among many gray white spotted leafy trees,
   I consumed jagged chunks of bark poisonous
   off of withered scaly limbs leprous.
And much later on in the journey I found a death city.

In the disease riddled darkness of an ancient
  necropolis, growing out of beds of black soil
  unctuous, I ingested odorous black banded fungus.
I did all of this on my way to get close,
  close to father Thanatos.

I became enclosed within father Thanatos's blackened
  wings, and heard the songs the Death Choir sings.
I moved not during the draining of my heated blood,
  nor yelled out while pained during the blackening of
  my bones.
And sometime soon I'll return to the noisy Upper
  Reality, to find you laughing and smiling in a false
  security.
And with my scythe gripped tight I'll visit you in the
  night, I'll make sure
  your head and body are connected no more.

The Mayfly Moons
By Shawn Vimislicky

Fantasy poetry at its finest, with new observations on classical literature, self-discovery, the longing for a better place (hiraeth), beings swept up in events, and fantasy romanticism. Often uplifting, sometimes darker, and here and there a mix of the two extremes, this collection will thrill you, haunt you, and raise your spirits.

Relics
Lee Clark Zumpe

No itinerarian shall pass through these gates,
This unnamed metropolis long inundated
By rising tides, forsaken by indifferent Fates;
Its populace, by misfortune, decimated.

Those hungry for tools of science and sorcery –
And other seekers of fortune, unwise and brave –
Have plunged 'neath the waves to plunder the
    sunken city
To join its long-dead denizens in their damp grave.

Still, its tallest towers and soaring spires survive,
Reaching from the depths to pierce the currents swift;
Fluids, strangely-hued, climb surfaceward, unalive,
And relics sometimes wash ashore amidst sea-drift.

Such tokens fetch coinage in port-city bazaars
Where collectors, nightly, seek bargains opportune
Beneath the meager mass of diminishing stars,
By the pallid glow of the sad and splintered moon.

Whispers from the Intoxicating Abyss
By Lee Clark Zumpe

You may not realize it, but they're out there: impossible shadows, omniscient horrors, and unseen, unknowable entities scattered across the great gulfs of nothingness at the edges of the universe. In this collection, author Lee Clark Zumpe draws back the curtain from the invisible realm, divulging its arcane secrets and ghastly revelations. Come walk paths meandering over shunned worlds adrift in darkness, and through seemingly mundane, liminal spaces that might be overrun with ancient shadows at any moment.

Stories are inspired by the works of H. P. Lovecraft.

Ordering links:

Print: https://www.hiraethsffh.com/product-page/whispers-from-the-intoxicating-abyss-by-lee-clark-zumpe

ePub: https://www.hiraethsffh.com/product-page/whispers-from-the-intoxicating-abyss-by-lee-clark-zumpe-2

PDF: https://www.hiraethsffh.com/product-page/whispers-from-the-intoxicating-abyss-by-lee-clark-zumpe-1

The Swamp Witch's Lament
Marcie Lynn Tentchoff

muck
mire
morass
your human
labels for my home
can not encompass all it means
to one who breathes the bogland vapors into magics
woven from a living realm of water, plant, and beast,
then wafts them towards you, hoping just
to pierce the smog of
your own world's
morass
mire

Bullet Cluster by John Dunphy
The master of scifaiku and haibun returns with this science fiction and fantasy collection in defense of minimalist poetry! Here he takes on modern social topics such as alien gender dysphoria, vampire gardeners, archeological digs, bounty hunters and portals, telepathy, and the difference between 'pray' and 'prey.' Come enjoy this foray into the Strange Side.
https://www.hiraethsffh.com/product-page/bullet-cluster-by-john-dunphy

A Scan of the Beating Heart
Hannah Marshall

Four worlds deep, the earth burns:
cave, sea, soil, sky.
A woman traps a butterfly in the cage of her palm,
its wings a failure of dust and silk.
A fish swims dead coral,
metal pilings carving marriage
with bedrock.
And inside the mausoleum of my lungs,
cloud hardens into sediment.
A trillion distant leaves, alight.
Wave after wave of laughter,
penguins diving from tall blue stones.
Daisies picked clean of their petals.
Four beats deep, the heart learns sorrow
is its first companion.
A breath, awake, and gravity
holds the body down.

Featured Poet: Dawn McCormack

Forever

As fire filled the pre-dawn sky
The earth shook and trembled,
Rocking, shifting, as frightened
Villagers streamed outside

It had been so long
We'd all but forgotten
Yet, the sudden loud explosion
Had called us from our slumber

To find that the great guardian above
Always there and always trusted
Had suddenly erupted in full fury
And now all we could do was flee

Yet as I tried to fling open my door
To join the others, the wooden barrier
Jammed, locking me inside, and,
In terror, I realized it was too late
Then, as the stifling heat choked my every
Breath, the blistering, vermilion lava,
Now racing down the once-verdant hillside,
Engulfed my home, my sanctuary

Mercifully, I lost consciousness as a thick
Darkness enveloped me, until finally,
When the boiling lava had cooled, hardening
Into a harsh, grey, ashen rock

My burning, reddened eyes opened
Miraculously, I had survived yet, crying
Out for help, only deafening silence answered
For now, in this endless night, I was truly alone

Desperately, I banged at the door and
Struck where the windows had been
For what seemed an endless eternity
And perhaps it really was, for it seemed

I was playing this same loop over and over
Clawing my way out through time and space
And, as you see, I'm still here, trapped
Forever in this cold dark place

nighttime travelling
pyramids loom, welcoming
me to life I knew

The Crimson Chamber

Digging, feverishly removing
Dirt from the darkened hillside
As the Perseids streak across
The midnight sky while a lone owl
Calls sonorously, and nearby
Tamaracks whisper their secrets

For several nights I've dreamed of
This magical place, hidden deep within
The earth, its velvet-carpeted stairway
Leading to a room with red velvet walls
Edged with golden curlicues, and statues
Of the goddess Bast set into carved recesses

At the far end of this glorious room is
An altar, upon which sits an even larger
Golden statue of Bast, a gold chalice and
Several other mystical tools, as well as
Gold coins engraved with hieroglyphics,
As well as Bast's likeness, also resting there

Now, fueled by this unlikely dream-driven
Obsession, I somehow know that, though
It makes no sense, tonight is the night that
I must find that fantastical chamber,
Enter it, and learn its secrets, regardless of
Whether I am ever able to return

And, so I dig, as the silver moon
Drifts westward and the Perseids
Slow their spectacular dance,
Knowing I could be slipping into
A dark madness, yet helpless
To abandon this rabid quest

not what you expect
Lee Clark Zumpe

It's not what you expect –
a fluttering veil, a rush of thoughts,
the soft voices of saintly overseers
conducting you into undiscovered regions.
The creak and thrum of the ship.
The sparkling white caps. The sea spray.
The gauzy clouds rolling overhead.
Moonbeams trail the wispy shrouds,
and you heed their counsel
when they ask you not to peer
beneath the gentle waves
where restless souls will meet your gaze.
In the distance lie the purple peaks
of an unnamed mountain range.
A safe harbor. A coastal village
with welcoming lodgings
and amiable storytellers
and the impossible vastness
of sparsely inhabited landscape.
It's not what you expect.

Minimalism:
A Handbook of Minimalist Genre Poetic Forms

This handbook contains articles about how to write various minimalist poetry forms such as scifaiku, senryu, sijo, haibun, empat perkataan, ghazals, cinquain, cherita, rengays, rengu, octains, tanka, threesomes, and many more. Each article is written by an expert in that particular poetry form.

Teri Santitoro, aka sakyu, who assembled this handbook, has been the editor of Scifaikuest since 2003.

https://www.hiraethsffh.com/product-page/minimalism-a-handbook-of-minimalist-genre-poetic-forms

The Richard E. Schell Page

first birth on mars
silent child
a simple gravestone

mars greenhouse
first roses bloom
nothing smelled so sweet

lasagna with cheese
in squeezable tube
a long way from earth

neighborhood great

big swirling gas pot
storm a furious red eye
mighty Jupiter

~ Denise Noe

Dissonance
Amy Grech

Social dissonance
breeds resistance.

So close, yet so
far. Six feet apart.
Breaks your heart.

You wear a mask
as a sign of respect.
One less person to infect.

Dreams deferred.
You forge ahead,
undeterred.

Tickets to the Apocalypse
Kendall Evans and David C. Kopaska-Merkel

We're selling tickets
to the apocalypse--
a limited time offer.
All the mega-movie stars
will be there, politicians
and paparazzi too
this is the big one, folks!

All the famous architects
and artists will be vying for
the best seats
to this final spectacle
Please note:
seating is limited
and the tickets are going fast!

You've seen spectacles before;
we were all thrilled to see
Mars swallowed up by
that experimental black hole
cutting the rings of Saturn loose
was a stunt we'll not soon forget
but never mind all that.

Astronomers are telling us
(these are truly stellar folks)
the portents we've been seeing
can only mean one thing

Surprise! The cosmos
is getting smaller every day
and now it won't be long

So cash in your life savings
and purchase a ticket!!!
So what if you're left destitute
There will be no repercussions
Other than the deep reverberations
of gravity waves turned inside out
As the Big Reverse Bang commences

Disclaimer: If, somehow, the apocalypse
should fail to occur or does not meet
your standards
or expectations
for the Gotterdammerung
there will be no refunds
whatsoever.

Mortals is another in a series of poetry collections by Shelly Bryant that is inspired by the Chinese concepts of Wuxing, or elements—in this case, Fire.

https://www.hiraethsffh.com/product-page/mortals-by-shelly-bryant

Identified
Marcie Lynn Tentchoff

My mom won't listen to me, but,
the deep trench through her cabbage patch,
the purple stains out on the stoop,
are not my fault.

She's fine with swapping stories with
old Mr. Branford down the street,
the tourists who want souvenirs,
and all the press.

She'll talk of greys, and crop designs,
of flashing lights, and tractor beams,
of abductees and anal probes;
with those she's fine.

But try to tell her all about
the squawking birds with glowing eyes
and metal beaks, and razor wings,
and she pooh-poohs.

She won't believe those spinning disks
that she accepts are truly real
are what those spacegulls love to eat...
and follow here.

Or that, like clams, those ufos
hide all their sweetest meat inside,
and dropping them on our front stoop

Lavinia and the Moon
Lee Clark Zumpe

It was neither in days of yore nor lands far afield –
and those who make that claim have been sadly misled –
that the Moon found himself hopelessly enamored
of an attractive, beguiling backstreet conjurer.
When my grandmother spoke of such things –
such as her many conversations with the melancholy
    troll
who found shelter beneath the Smithfield Street Bridge;
or her adventures with the tortoise-shell cat
who shelved books at the Carnegie Library of Pittsburgh
–
she did so without a hint of rhapsody and hyperbole,
but with a sort of solemn nostalgic affection.
This comely enchanter, as I recall, worked the carnival
    circuit
through much of the year, settling in the winter months
with a cluster of relatives in a downtown tenement.
My grandmother knew her as Lavinia –
though she changed her name as often as her hairstyle.
One December she met a rugged steel-worker
in a crowded speakeasy at the Omni William Penn Hotel.
Some say the sorceress resorted to witchcraft –
assorted charms and amulets, potions and rituals –
to arouse his desire and diminish inhibition.
My grandmother said she needed no such contrivances
having been blessed with uncanny charm and beauty.
Their love affair, sadly, was short-lived:
He died in the steel mill, asphyxiated by furnace gas.
Lavinia's grief sent her to the Smithfield Street Bridge
beneath cloudless skies one starry night in January,
and she gazed into the black churning waters
of the Monongahela River, its currents and eddies,

and her tears fell like sparkling diamonds in moonlight.
My grandmother says it was her heartache or devotion
that first attracted the attention of that icy Moon,
whose face – reflected on the surface of the water –
furrowed with ripples at her lamentation.
The Moon fell upon her, and pale white flowers bloomed.
The Moon enveloped her, sheltering her in silvery light.
The Moon illuminated her, offering comfort and
    compassion.
No one saw Lavinia after her midnight sojourn –
though most agreed the black churning waters
had taken advantage of her sorrows
and invited her to step into those grim currents
    and eddies.
Not so, said the melancholy troll who resides
along the riverbank beneath the Smithfield Street Bridge:
He confirmed that the Moon swathed her in his radiance,
And scooped her out of the torrent of darkness.
No one thought to ask him – except for my grandmother.

www.ingramcontent.com/pod-product-compliance
Lightning Source LLC
LaVergne TN
LVHW020420070526
838199LV00055B/3674